INDIAN CUISINE
Slow Oven Dishes

INDIAN ✳ CUISINE

✳ Slow Oven Dishes ✳

Tiger Books International

London

Acknowledgement:
*Grateful thanks to Madhu Arora, Kiran Kapoor and Mili Paul
for having tried, tested and making available
the dishes for photography.*

ISBN: 1-85501-814-4

© Lustre Press Pvt. Ltd. 1996

This edition published in 1996 by:
Tiger Books International PLC, Twickenham

Project Coordinator:
Arti Arora

Production:
N.K. Nigam, Gautam Dey, Abhijeet Raha

Conceived & Designed by:
Pramod Kapoor
at
Roli Books CAD Centre

Photographer:
Dheeraj Paul

Other photographs by:
Neeraj Paul: page 32

Printed and bound by:
Star Standard Industries Pte. Ltd., Singapore

CONTENTS

———— * ————

7

To get you acquainted...

9

Spices—The Sweet & Sour of Indian Food

10

Basic Indian Recipes

11

Chicken

29

Lamb

47

Seafood

59

Vegetables

75

Accompaniments and Desserts

84

Index

▲ *Kadhai* (Wok)

Belan (Rolling pin) - *Chakla* (Flour board)

Tawa (Griddle) ▶

Chimta (Tongs)

Kaddoo kas (Grater) ▼

Masaaldaan (Spice container) ▶

Hamam dasta (Mortar pestle) ▼

Handi (Heavy-bottomed pot) ▼

Karchi (Ladles) ▶

Pateela (Deep pot) ▼

TO GET YOU AQUAINTED.....

Slow Oven or *Dum Pukht* has become one of the most refined forms of cooking in India, even though the style is no more than 200 years old. A culinary fable has it, that Nawab Wajid Ali Shah of Lucknow was touring a construction when he happened to pass by a huge cauldron, being unsealed to feed the workers. In that fire-stoked cauldron, were meats, vegetables and spices and when the the lid was lifted off, Wajid Ali Shah found himself inhaling the aromas of a gourmet heaven. And so in the 'twixt of an eye, royal chefs were trained to recreate the experience in the royal kitchens and a legendary cuisine was born.

Slow Oven means cooking on very low flame, mostly in sealed containers, allowing the meats and vegetables to cook, as far as possible, in their own juices. The spices used are less than those in traditional Indian cooking, with fresh spices and herbs for flavouring. In some cases, cooking dough is spread over the container, like a lid, to seal the foods. This is known as a *purdah* (veil), but on cooking becomes a bread which has absorbed the flavours of the food and the two are, therefore, best eaten together. In the end, *Dum Pukht* food is about aroma, when the seal is broken on the table and the fragrance of a Lucknavi repast floats in the air . . . .

Indian cuisine has a range and variety that is extraordinary, with each region contributing its own flavour. Modern Indian cooking borrows selectively from these diverse styles, assimilates and adapts them to suit the palate. The richness of Indian food, therefore continues to grow.

Regional differences in food are often so great that they make for entirely different cuisines. What is common are the raw ingredients, the vegetables and meats, and the spices. But, while the greater part of India is vegetarian, there are other regions where meat and chicken are considered an essential part of the daily meal. In Bengal, fish is an obsession and is referred to as *jal toru*, an underwater vegetable.

Indian food is usually eaten without starters, soups or courses, though in restaurants it is presented in this manner for less familiar diners. The main meal is eaten with either rice or *rotis* and includes at least one lentil curry called daal, a selection of vegetarian servings, a meat, chicken or fish fry, a sampling of chutneys and pickles, and *dahi* (yoghurt). *Papads* are served with meals that maybe sometimes accompanied by *lassi* (buttermilk) which helps to induce sleep on a warm afternoon! Desserts are not standard. Sweets, of course, are served with almost any Indian meal and may take the form of a South Indian *halwa*, a delicate Lucknavi *kheer* or light Bengali sweets. But, depending on the region, these may be served after, during or before an Indian meal. No wonder Indian food continues to surprise its serving and style almost as variable as its thousands of recipes.

Tej patta (Bay leaves)   *Methi dana* (Fenugreek seed)   *Khus khus* (Poppy seeds)   *Ajwain* (Carom seeds)   *Javitri* (Mace)

Raee (Mustard seeds)   *Haldi* (Turmeric powder)   *Choti elaichi* (Green cardamom)   *Heeng* (Asafoetida)   *Laung* (Cloves)

Bari elaichi (Black cardamom)   *Amchur* (Green mango powder)   *Laal mirch* (Red chilli)   *Dhania* (Coriander) *powder*   *Kaali mirch* (Black peppercor

SPICES — THE SWEET & SOUR OF INDIAN FOOD

The secret of Indian cuisine lies in its spices. Used lightly but in exciting combinations, they can leave the palate tingling for more, without actually taking a toll on one's digestion.

As the story goes, the West had discovered and traded with pockets of the Indian subcontinent, primarily for its rich spices.

Although, the beneficial uses of spices have been recorded in ancient treatises, but the usage has known to vary from region to region. Apart from making food palatable, spices also have inherent 'cooling' and 'warming' properties. They are added to the foods intended for pregnant women, for invalids, for the old and of course for the very young, to aid recovery or to impart stamina.

The basic Indian spices alongwith salt, are *jeera* (**cumin**) to impart fragrance to food, *haldi* (*turmeric*) to give colour and *laal mirch* (**red chilli**) to spice up the food. *Amchur* (*dry mango powder*) adds piquancy and a mere pinch of *heeng* (**asafoetida**) adds a unique taste and also aids digestion. Fresh **coriander** is the most common garnish and also adds a light fragrance.

Since fruits are seen as energy-giving, **dried fruits** are used extensively in India. Parts of fruits, berries or vegetables are dried and stored, as condiments. Several seeds too are used, each with a marked taste.

Saunf (**fennel**) is added to desserts and some vegetarian dishes to act as a flavouring agent. *Methi dana* (**fenugreek seeds**) gives a touch of bitterness, *kalonji* (**onion seeds**) is used in 'heavier' cooking or for pickles. *Raee* (**mustard seeds**) adds sourness to food while *khus-khus* (**poppy seeds**) enhances the flavour of meat. Fresh *imli* (**tamarind**) imparts a sour taste and *kesar* (**saffron**), India's most expensive herb, imparts a fine fragrance alongwith a rich yellow colour.

That Indian spices can be used almost in any fashion and to enhance any taste, is obvious from the fact that Indian tea too uses spices!! *Elaichi* (**cardamom**) is added to tea for flavouring, while saffron and almonds are added to *kahwa* (Kashmiri tea).

9

BASIC INDIAN RECIPES

Coconut chutney: Grated **coconut** (160 gms), roasted **gram** (15 gms), **curry leaves** (8), **green chillies,** chopped (5), **ginger,** chopped (15 gms), **lentils (*urad daal*),** (5 gms), **mustard seeds** (5 gms), **oil** (15 ml) and **salt** (to taste). Grind coconut, green chillies, ginger and gram to a paste. Sauté mustard seeds, lentils and curry leaves. Stir in the ground paste, cook for 3-5 minutes. Allow to cool, refrigerate and use when required.

Garam masala (for 445 gms): Finely grind the following ingredients and store: **cumin seeds** (90 gms), **black pepper corns** (70 gms), **black cardamom seeds** (75 gms), **fennel seeds** (30 gms), **green cardamoms** (40 gms), **coriander seeds** (30 gms), **cloves** (20 gms), **cinnamon sticks** (20 x 2.5 cm), **mace powder** (20 gms), **black cumin seeds** (20 gms), **dry rose petals** (15 gms), **bay leaves** (15 gms), **ginger powder** (15 gms).

Ginger paste or **Garlic paste:** Soak **ginger / garlic cloves** (300 gms) overnight to soften the skin. Peel and chop roughly. Process until pulped. The pulp can be stored in an airtight container and refrigerated for 4-6 weeks.

Green Chilli paste: Take required quantity of **green chillies**, chop roughly and process until pulped.

Khoya: Boil **milk** (2 lts) in a *kadhai* (wok). Simmer till quantity is reduced to half, stirring occasionally. Continue cooking, now stirring constantly and scraping from the sides, till a thick paste-like consistency is obtained (1-1½ hrs.). Allow to cool.

Mint Chutney: Mint leaves (60 gms), **coriander leaves** (120 gms), **cumin seeds** (5 gms), **garlic cloves** (2), **green chilli** (1), **raw mango** (30 gms), **tomatoes** (45 gms), **salt** (to taste). Chop all ingredients, blend until paste-like. Refrigerate in an airtight container.

Onion paste: Peel and chop the **onions** (500 gms) in quarters. Process until pulped. Refrigerate in an airtight container for 4-6 weeks. For **Browned Onion Paste**, slice and fry the onions in a little oil, allow to cool before processing.

Paneer (Cottage Cheese): In a pot, put **milk** (3 lts) to boil. Just before it boils, add (90 ml/6 tbs) **lemon juice / vinegar** to curdle the milk. Strain the curdled milk through a muslin cloth, to allow all whey and moisture to drain. Still wrapped in the muslin, place **paneer** under a weight for 2-3 hours to allow to set into a block which can be cut or grated.

CHICKEN

Slow Oven Tandoori Chicken (recipe on following page) ▶

Slow Oven Tandoori Chicken

White rice

Serves: 4-5   Preparation time: 40 minutes   Cooking time: 20 minutes
+ 6 hours for tandoori chicken

Ingredients:

For tandoori chicken
Chicken broiler (skinless)
(600 gms each) 2
Salt to taste
Red chilli paste .... *25 gms / 5 tsp*
Ginger paste (page 10) .... *10 gms / 2 tsp*
Garlic paste (page 10) ....*50 gms / 3¹/₃ tbs*
Lemon juice .... *30 ml / 2 tbs*

For the marinade:
Yoghurt, drained .... *200 gms / 1 cup*
Cumin (*jeera*) powder .... *5 gms / 1 tsp*
Garam masala (page 10) .... *10 gms / 2 tsp*
Ginger paste (page 10) .... *25 gms / 5 tsp*

Lemon juice .... *30 ml / 2 tbs*
Oil .... *50 ml / 3¹/₃ tbs*
Saffron (*kesar*) .... *few strands*

For the (covering) dough:
Butter (melted) .... *50 gms / ¹/₄ cup*
Flour .... *150 gms / ³/₄ cup*
Salt to taste
Sugar .... *10 gms / 2 tsp*
Milk .... *100 ml / ¹/₂ cup*
Vetivier (*kewda*) essence .... *2 drops*
Cream .... *120 ml / 2 ²/₃ cup*
Egg (yolks only) 2

Method:

1. Make incisions on breasts, thighs and legs of chicken.
2. Mix the salt, red chilli paste, ginger-garlic pastes and lemon juice, rub into the chicken. Keep aside for 30 minutes.
3. Whisk yoghurt in a bowl, mix all ingredients for marinade. Coat chicken with marinade and refrigerate for 5-6 hours.
4. Preheat the oven or tandoor to 175 °C (350 °F).
5. Roast approximately for 15 minutes or until almost done. Keep aside.
6. Grease two casserole dishes, one for each chicken.
7. Sieve the flour and salt in a mixing bowl.
8. Dissolve sugar in warm milk, add the vetivier and stir. Pour this into the flour, knead into a dough and keep aside for 15 minutes.
9. Add butter to the dough, knead again and keep aside for 10 minutes.
10. Divide dough into two equal portions, shape into balls and dust with flour. Keep aside for another 5 minutes.
11. Roll out the balls into discs, the size of each casserole dish. Prick the surface of the disc with a fork.

◀ *Picture on preceding page*

13. Preheat the oven to 150 °C (350 °F).
14. Cut each chicken into 4 pieces and arrange them in the casserole. Drizzle cream on each chicken and cover the dish with the rolled out disc to make a covering (*parda*). Press the edges to seal and brush the top with beaten egg yolk.
15. Bake for 10-15 minutes, until the covering is golden brown.
16. Cut open the covering (*parda*) and serve the chicken alongwith one portion of the covering (*parda*).

Chicken Mince Rolls

Serves: 8   Preparation time: 15 minutes   Cooking time: 30 minutes

Ingredients:

Cabbage (large) *1*

For the filling:

Chicken, minced .... *550 gms*
Ginger, chopped .... *10 gms / 2 tsp*
Garlic, chopped .... *10 gms / 2 tsp*
Onion, chopped .... *20 gms / 4 tsp*
Green chilli, chopped .... *5 gms / 1 tsp*
Green cardamom (*choti elaichi*) powder
.... *2 gms / ¼ tsp*
Cloves (*laung*) powder .... *1.5 gms / ¼ tsp*
Red chilli paste .... *5 gms / 1 tsp*
Almond paste .... *15 gms / 1 tbs*

Salt to taste

For the curry:

Butter ....*40 gms / 2 ⅔ tbs*
Onion paste (page 10) ....*50 gms / 3 ⅔ tsp*
Yellow chilli powder .... *8 gms / 1 ½ tbs*
Turmeric (*haldi*) powder .... *a pinch*
Cumin (*jeera*) powder .... *3 gms / ½ tsp*
Coriander powder .... *4 gms / ¾ tsp*
Saffron (*kesar*) .... *1 gms / a pinch*
Garam masala (page 10) .... *3 gms / ½ tsp*
Coconut milk .... *200 ml / 1 cup*
Cream .... *150 ml / ¾ cup*

Method:

1. Cut the stem and blanch the cabbage.
2. **For the filling**, mix all ingredients and divide into 8 equal portions.
3. Spread out 2 cabbage leaves, place one portion of filling in the centre and make a roll. Make eight such rolls.
4. **For the curry**, Heat butter in a *handi* (pot). Sauté onion paste, add spices and cook till the oil separates.
5. Place the cabbage rolls carefully in the *handi* (pot) and pour the coconut milk and cream. Cover with lid and seal the edges with dough and let it cook in a moderately hot oven for 20 minutes.
6. Remove from the oven, serve hot, accompanied by a green salad.

Chicken Drumsticks in a unique marinade

Serves: 4-5   Preparation time: 45 minutes   Cooking time: 20 minutes

Ingredients:

Chicken drumsticks 4
Chicken, minced .... 300 gms
Garlic paste (page 10) .... 25 gms / 5 tsp
Ginger paste (page 10) .... 25 gms / 5 tsp
Salt to taste
Green chilli paste (page 10) ..... 25 gms / 5 tsp
Lemon juice .... 30 ml / 2 tbs

Almonds .... 50 gms / $3^1/_3$ tbs
Cashewnuts .... 50 gms / $3^1/_3$ tbs
Mint chutney (page 10) .... 100 gms / ½ cup
Garam masala (page 10) .... 5 gms / 1 tsp
Saffron (kesar) .... a pinch
Groundnut oil .... 15 ml / 1 tbs
Cream .... 100 ml / ½ cup

Method:

1. Debone the entire chicken leg, leaving only the top of the drumstick. Flatten the chicken leg using a steak hammer.

2. Make a marinade with half the quantity of ginger and garlic paste, salt, green chilli paste and lemon juice. Marinate the chicken in this and refrigerate for half an hour.

3. Mix the almonds and cashewnuts with the chicken mince and chutney.

4. Add garam masala and the remaining ginger, garlic, green chilli pastes, salt and lemon juice to the mince mixture and mix well.

5. Stuff the deboned chicken with this mixture, rolling the chicken in such a way that the mince is wrapped in it.

6. Grease a baking tray with groundnut oil. Place the rolls on the tray and cover with foil. Bake in a medium oven to 100 °C (200 °F) until done (approximately 20 minutes).

7. Take the chicken out of the oven and remove the foil. Slice each chicken roll diagonally and arrange on a platter.

8. Pour the saffron mixed with cream over the sliced chicken.

9. Serve hot, accompanied by a green salad.

Slow Oven Chicken with a hint of Mint

Serves: 4-5   Preparation time: 15 minutes   Cooking time: 30 minutes

Ingredients:

Chicken (small) boneless cubes .... *1 kg*	Turmeric (*haldi*) powder .... *5 gms / 1 tsp*
Oil ....*25 ml / 1²/₃ tbs*	Red chilli powder .... *10 gms / 2 tsp*
Butter (unsalted) .... *25 gms / 5 tsp*	Salt to taste
Bay leaf (*tej patta*) *1*	Almond paste .... *100 gms / ½ cup*
Cinnamon (*daalchini*) sticks *5*	Cream .... *120 ml / ²/₃ cup*
Cloves (*laung*) *6*	Green chillies, slit into half *6*
Green cardamoms (*choti elaichi*) *10*	Mace (*javitri*) powder .... *3 gms / ²/₃ tsp*
Onions, grated...................... *180 gms / ³/₅ cup*	Vetivier (*kewda*) essence .... *3 drops*
Ginger paste (page 10) .... *25 gms / 5 tsp*	Mint leaves, (fresh) .... *5 gms / 1 tsp*
Garlic paste (page 10) .... *25 gms / 5 tsp*	

Method:

1. Heat the oil and butter in a pan. Add bay leaf, cinnamon, cloves and cardamoms and sauté over medium heat until they begin to crackle.

2. Add the onions and sauté for few minutes. Add the ginger and garlic pastes, turmeric, red chilli powder, salt and almond paste and cook over medium heat for 5-10 minutes until the oil separates from the mixture.

3. Add the chicken, stir and cook over medium heat for 10-15 minutes.

4. Add the cream, green chillies, mace powder and vetivier.

5. Sprinkle with fresh mint leaves, cover and seal lid with dough. Let the chicken simmer over very low heat for 5-6 minutes. It could also be kept in a slow oven for 10 minutes.

6. Garnish with chopped coriander and chopped whole red chillies (optional) and serve hot, accompanied by Lachha Parantha (page 76).

Chicken Handi

Serves: 4   Preparation: 20 minutes   Cooking: 30 minutes

Ingredients:

Chicken (thighs), boneless .... *800 gms*
Saffron (*kesar*) .... *1 gms / a pinch*
Oil .... *75 ml / 5 tbs*
Garlic, chopped .... *30 gms / 2 tbs*
Onions, sliced .... *90 gms / ¹/₃ cup*
Cinnamon (*daalchini*) .... *1" stick*
Cloves (*laung*) *10*

Green cardamoms (*choti elaichi*) *4*
Ginger paste (page 10) .... *20 gms / 4 tsp*
Garlic paste (page 10) .... *20 gms / 4 tsp*
Salt to taste
Yellow chilli powder .... *2.5 gms / ¹/₂ tsp*
Chicken stock .... *¹/₂ litre / 2 cups*

Method:

1. Cut chicken into small pieces.

2. Soak saffron in a spoonful of water for 10 minutes. Crush and keep aside.

3. Heat oil in a saucepan and add chopped garlic. Sauté till brown. Add the onions and sauté till light brown.

4. Add cinnamon, cloves and cardamoms and sauté till the onions turn golden brown.

5. Add the ginger and garlic pastes, chicken, salt and yellow chilli powder. Stir for 3-4 minutes. Add chicken stock and bring to boil. Cover and simmer till chicken is tender.

6. Remove from fire. Take out the chicken pieces from the gravy. Strain the gravy into another pot through a soup strainer.

7. Cook the gravy till it is reduced to a sauce-like consistency. Add the chicken pieces and cook for a minute.

8. Stir in the prepared saffron, remove from heat and serve hot, accompanied by an Indian bread of your choice.

Tamarind flavoured Chicken

Serves: 4   Preparation time: 1 hour   Cooking time: 45 minutes

Ingredients:

Chicken .... *1.2 kg*	Onions, chopped .... *85 gms / $1/_3$ cup*
Red chilli powder .... *2.5 gms / ½ tsp*	Green cardamom (*choti elaichi*) powder
Turmeric (*haldi*) powder .... *5 gms / 1 tsp*	.... *2.5 gms / ½ tsp*
Salt to taste	Clove (*laung*) powder .... *1.25 gms / ¼ tsp*
Garlic paste (page 10) .... *30 gms / 2 tbs*	Coriander powder .... *2.5 gms / ½ tsp*
Ginger paste (page 10) .... *45 gms / 3 tbs*	Cinnamon (*daalchini*) powder
Groundnut oil .... *80 ml / $1/_3$ cup*	.... *1.25 gms / ¼ tsp*
Tamarind (*imlee*) .... *25 gms / 5 tsp*	Black peppercorns, pounded *2.5 gms / ½ tsp*
Curry leaves *12*	Green coriander, chopped .... *20 gms / 4 tsp*
Tomatoes, chopped .... *120 gms / ½ cup*	Lemon juice .... *15 ml / 1 tbs*

Method:

1. Clean the chicken, debone and cut into 1½ inch cubes.
2. Mix red chillies, turmeric and salt with half of the ginger and garlic pastes. Rub this marinade into the chicken pieces. Keep aside for 30 minutes.
3. Heat oil in a *kadhai*(wok), add the marinated chicken and sauté over medium heat until light brown from all sides.
4. Remove chicken and reserve the oil.
5. Soak tamarind in a cup of water. After 10 minutes, mash well, squeeze out the pulp and discard. Keep extract aside.
6. Reheat the reserved oil, add curry leaves and stir over medium heat for 30 seconds. Add onions and sauté until light brown. Add the remaining ginger and garlic pastes, stir for a minute, add tomatoes and stir. Cook till the fat appears on the sides of the pan. Add cardamom, coriander, clove and cinnamon powders and stir for a minute. Add the tamarind and cook for 5 minutes.
7. Add chicken pieces and simmer for 8-10 minutes. Add water (1 cup) and bring to boil. Reduce heat to medium and cook, stirring constantly until the moisture has evaporated and the chicken pieces are coated evenly.
8. Sprinkle pepper and lemon juice.
9. Remove to a flat dish, garnish with green coriander and onion rings. Serve hot, accompanied by Lachha Parantha (page 76).

Tangy Chicken

Serves: 4   Preparation time: 45 minutes   Cooking time: 30 minutes

Ingredients:

Chicken breasts *12*
Yoghurt .... *240 gms / 1¼ cup*
Garlic paste (page 10) .... *20 gms / 4 tsp*
Ginger paste (page 10) .... *20 gms / 4 tsp*
Cumin (*jeera*) seeds .... *5 gms / 1 tsp*
Black pepper powder .... *5 gms / 1 tsp*
Lemon juice .... *30 ml / 2 tbs*
Green chillies, chopped *4*

Almond paste .... *45 gms / 3 tbs*
Onions, cut in strips .... *160 gms / ²/₃ cup*
Capsicum, cut in strips .... *100 gms*
Saffron (*kesar*) dissolved in 1 tbs milk
.... *a pinch,*
Salt to taste
Butter (unsalted) .... *60 gms / 4 tbs*

Method:

1. Hang yoghurt in a muslin cloth to drain all whey.

2. Clean and debone chicken breasts.

3. Make a marinade of yoghurt, ginger and garlic pastes, salt, cumin, black pepper, lemon, juice, green chillies and almond paste. Marinate the chicken in it for half an hour.

4. Grease an oven-proof shallow dish. Place the chicken pieces in it, without overlapping. Arrange the onion and capsicum rings over the chicken pieces and pour the left-over marinade evenly over it.

5. Dot with dollops of butter and roast in a preheated oven at 150 °C (300 °F) for 20 minutes.

6. Remove, sprinkle saffron, cover with aluminium and simmer in the oven for another 10 minutes.

7. Remove from the oven, transfer to a serving platter. Garnish with capsicum strips (optional). Serve simmering hot, accompanied by Lachha Parantha (page 76).

◀ *Tangy Chicken*

Chicken in a Spinach Purée

Serves: 4-5   Preparation time: 10 minutes   Cooking time: 45 minutes

Ingredients:

Chicken, skinned cut into pieces .... *1 kg*
Oil .... *60 ml / 4 tbs*
Cinnamon (*daalchini*) sticks *4*
Bay leaves (*tej patta*) *2*
Ginger paste (page 10) .... *40 gms / 2²/₃ tbs*
Garlic paste (page 10) .... *40 gms / 2²/₃ tbs*
Onion paste (page 10) .... *200 gms / 1 cup*
Red chilli powder .... *10 gms / 2 tsp*
Tomatoes, chopped .... *180 gms / ³/₄ cup*

Spinach (*palak*), puréed .. *350 gms / 1³/₄ cups*
Maizeflour (*makke ka atta*) .... *3 gms /²/₃ tsp*
Water .... *40 ml / 2²/₃ tbs*
Butter .... *100 gms / ¹/₂ cup*
Salt to taste
White pepper powder .... *3 gms /²/₃ tsp*
Ginger, julienned .... *10 gms / 2 tsp*
Fenugreek (*methi*) powder .... *3 gms /²/₃ tsp*

Method:

1. Heat oil in a pan, add cinnamon and bay leaves and sauté over medium heat until they begin to crackle.

2. Add the ginger, garlic and onion pastes and red chilli powder, sauté for 30-60 seconds.

3. Add tomatoes and sauté further for 1 minute.

4. Stir in the spinach purée and the maize flour (diluted with water) and cook over medium heat for 10-15 minutes, stirring occasionally.

5. In another pan, heat the butter and sauté the chicken until lightly browned.

6. Transfer the chicken pieces into the spinach purée. Add salt and white pepper powder, cover and simmer on very low heat (*dum*) for 10-15 minutes or till chicken is cooked.

7. Serve hot, garnished with chopped whole red chillies (optional) and fenugreek powder, accompanied by Naan (page 77).

Saffron Chicken

Serves: 4   Preparation time: 20 minutes   Cooking time: 35 minutes

Ingredients:

Chicken boneless, cut into 8 pcs ...... *800 gms*
Oil .... *100 ml / ½ cup*
Bay leaves (*tej patta*) *2*
Cloves (*laung*) *6*
Green cardamoms (*choti elaichi*) *6*
Onion paste (page 10) .... *160 gms / ¾ cup*
Ginger paste (page 10) .... *30 gms / 2 tbs*
Garlic paste (page 10) .... *30 gms / 2 tbs*

Coriander powder .... *6 gms / 1 tsp*
Cashewnut paste .... *75 gms / 5 tbs*
Yoghurt, whisked .... *225 gms / 1 cup*
Salt to taste
White pepper powder .... *3 gms / 1 tsp*
Saffron (*kesar*) .... *a pinch*
Cream .... *150 ml / ¾ cup*

Method:

1. Heat oil in a heavy bottomed pan. Add bay leaf, cloves and cardamom and sauté until the cardamom changes colour.
2. Add onion paste, ginger and garlic pastes and stir-fry till the oil separates.
3. Add coriander powder and cashewnut paste, stir-fry for 2 minutes.
4. Add chicken pieces and cook for 3 minutes.
5. Mix in the yoghurt, add salt, white pepper and saffron.
6. Bring to boil, reduce heat, simmer until chicken becomes tender.
7. Garnish with chopped coriander and slit-green chillies (optional). Serve hot, accompanied by any Indian bread.

Chicken Drumsticks

Serves: 3-4   Preparation time: 4 ½ hours   Cooking time: 30-40 minutes

Ingredients:

Chicken drumsticks .... *800 gms*
For the marinade:
Ginger paste (page 10) .... *10 gms / 2 tsp*
Garlic paste (page 10) .... *10 gms / 2 tsp*
Lemon juice .... *30 ml / 2 tbs*
Salt
Red chilli paste .... *10 gms / 2 tsp*
Garam masala (page 10) .... *3 gms / ½ tsp*

Yoghurt, drained .... *100 gms / ½ cup*
Coriander powder .... *10 gms / 2 tsp*
Yoghurt .... *200 gms / 1 cup*
Brown onion paste (page 10)   *60 gms / 4 tbs*
Cumin (*jeera*) seeds .... *20 gms / 4 tsp*
Black peppercorns .... *15 gms / 1 tbs*
Green coriander, chopped .... *20 gms / 4 tsp*

◀ *Saffron Chicken*

Method:

1. Make 3 incisions on each drumstick.
2. Whisk together, the ingredients for the marinade.
3. Rub marinade into the drumsticks and leave aside for 4 hours.
4. Skewer the drumsticks and roast in a tandoor for 8-10 minutes.
5. Remove from skewers and place drumsticks in oven- proof dish mixed with the rest of the ingredients. Cover tightly and bake for 25 minutes. Alternatively, cook it in a *handi* (pot), sealed with dough over a hot plate for 30 minutes on low heat.

Spicy Chicken Curry

Serves:5-6   Preparation time: 4-5 hours   Cooking time: 1 hour

Ingredients:

For the marinade:

Chicken (350g each), skinned 4
Ginger paste (page 10) .... *20 gms / 4 tsp*
Garlic paste (page 10) .... *20 gms / 4 tsp*
Red chilli powder .... *5 gms / 1 tsp*
Turmeric (*haldi*) powder ....*2 gms / ¹/₃ tsp*
Salt to taste

For the filling:

Chicken, minced .... *200 gms*
Onions (sautéed) .... *30 gms / 2 tbs*
Ginger, finely chopped .... *10 gms / 2 tsp*
Peppercorns (crushed) .... *3 gms / ¹/₂ tsp*
Black cumin (*shah jeera*) .... *a pinch*
Green cardamom (*choti elaichi*) *4*

Coriander powder .... *3 gms / ¹/₂ tsp*
Fennel (*saunf*) powder ....*2 gms / ¹/₃ tsp*
Almonds, chopped finely *10*
Pistachios, chopped finely *20*
Cashewnut, chopped finely *1*

For the curry:

Yoghurt ....*250 ml / 1¹/₄ cup*
Red chilli powder .... *5 gms / 1 tsp*
Salt to taste
Almond paste .... *25 gms / 5 tsp*
Mace (*javitri*) powder ....*2 gms / ¹/₃ tsp*
Green cardamom (*choti elaichi*) *5*
Butter.. *60 gms / 4 tbs*

Method:

1. Clean the chicken, marinate with ginger-garlic pastes, red chilli, turmeric and salt for 4 hours.
2. **For the filling**, mix all the ingredients and divide into 4 parts. Stuff the stomach cavity of each chicken with one portion of filling.
3. Skewer the chickens and roast in a tandoor or in a very hot oven for 8-10 minutes.
4. Whisk together all the ingredients for the curry.
5. Place the chicken in a *handi* (pot)or an oven-proof dish, alongwith the yogurt mixture and cook on low heat for 25-30 minutes. Serve hot, accompanied by any Indian bread.

LAMB

Slow Oven Lamb Steaks *(recipe on following page)* ▶

Slow Oven Lamb Steaks

Serves: 4   Preparation time: 30 minutes   Cooking time: 45 minutes

Ingredients:

Lamb escallops (2" × 4") .... *750 gms*
Oil .... *120 ml / ½ cup*
Onions, sliced .... *240 gms / 1 cup*
Ginger .... *25 gms / 1 sq" piece*
Garlic cloves .... *45 gms / 3 tbs*
Poppy (*khus khus*) seeds .... *15 gms / 1 tbs*
Black cardamoms (*bari elaichi*) *2*
Cinnamon (*daalchini*) .... *1" stick*
Bay leaf (*tej patta*) *1*

Cloves (*laung*) *6*
Yoghurt .... *240 gms / 1 ¹/₃ cup*
Red chilli powder .... *5 gms / 1 tsp*
Garam masala (page 10) .... *5 gms / 1 tsp*
Green cardamom (*choti elaichi*) powder
.... *2.5 gms / ½ tsp*
Black pepper powder .... *2.5 gms / ½ tsp*
Green coriander, chopped .... *5 gms / 1 tsp*

Method:

1. Heat oil in a *kadhai* (wok) and sauté the onions till golden brown. Remove and keep aside.
2. Peel and chop the ginger and garlic.
3. Blend the ginger, garlic, onion and poppy seeds alongwith water (2 tbs) to make a paste.
4. Reheat the remaining oil in *kadhai* (wok), sauté the black cardamoms, cinnamon, bay leaf and cloves till they crackle. Add blended paste and cook for 3-4 minutes.
5. Stir in the yoghurt and cook for 4-5 minutes. Add the lamb pieces and cook for another 3-4 minutes, till the oil separates.
6. Transfer to a casserole and add water (½ cup). Sprinkle red chilli powder, garam masala, cardamom powder and black pepper. Cover and cook in a preheated (275 °F) oven for 10 minutes.
7. Serve hot, garnished with chopped coriander and accompanied by Naan (page 77).

◀ *Picture on preceding page*

Lamb Curry

Serves: 4-5   Preparation time: 2 hours   Cooking time: 1 hour

Ingredients:

Lamb leg (cut into pieces) .... *800 gms*
Ginger paste (page 10) .... *10 gms / 2 tsp*
Garlic paste (page 10) .... *15 gms / 1 tbs*
Salt to taste
Oil .... *100 ml / ½ cup*
Onions, sliced .... *350 gms / 1 ¾ cup*
Cloves (*laung*) *6*
Cardamom (*elaichi*) *6*
Mace (*javitri*) *3*
Cinnamon (*daalchini*) stick *1*

Coriander powder .... *20 gms / 4 tsp*
Red chilli powder .... *15 gms / 1 tbs*
Tomatoes, blanched, skinned, chopped
.... 500 gms
Yoghurt .... *200 gms*
Chironji paste .... *30 gms / 2 tbs*
Almond paste .... *20 gms / 4 tsp*
Saffron (*kesar*) .... *1 gm*
Green coriander, ... *10 gms / 2 tsp*

Method:

1. Marinate lamb with ginger and garlic pastes and salt. Keep aside for 2 hours.

2. Heat oil in a heavy-bottomed pan, add onion, cloves, cardamom, mace and cinnamon. Stir-fry till the onion becomes tender. Add coriander powder and red chilli powder. Stir-fry for a few minutes and remove from heat.

3. Transfer to an oven-proof dish and add the tomatoes, yoghurt, chironji paste, almond paste and saffron.

4. Cover the dish with a layer of dough and cook in an oven for about 35 minutes.

5. Remove from oven and serve hot, garnished with chopped coriander and accompanied by Naan (page 77) and Boondi Raita (page 81).

Boneless Lamb in Tomato Purée

Serves: 4   Preparation time: ½ hour   Cooking time: 1 ½ hours

Ingredients:

Lamb (cut into boneless cubes) ...... *900 gms*
Oil .... *125 ml / ²/₃ cup*
Cinnamon (*daalchini*) sticks *2*
Cloves (*laung*) *5*
Nutmeg (*jaiphal*) .... *a pinch*
Green cardamoms (*choti elaichi*) *4*
Ginger-Garlic paste (page 10)
.... *40 gms / 2 ½ tbs*
Onions, chopped .... *200 gms / 1 cup*
Salt .... *8 gms / 1 ½ tsp*
Red chilli powder .... *5 gms / 1 tsp*
Coriander powder .... *5 gms / 1 tsp*

Turmeric (*haldi*) powder .... *5 gms / 1 tsp*
Carrots (cut into rounds) .... *200 gms / 1 cup*
Tomato purée, fresh .... *200 gms / 1 cup*
Khoya (page 10) .... *30 gms / 2 tbs*
Brown onion paste (page10)
.... *40 gms / 2 ½ tbs*
Green peas, shelled .... *100 gms / ½ cup*
Mushroom (stems removed)
.... *80 gms / ¹/₃ cup*
Cashewnuts, whole .... *150 gms / ²/₃ cup*
Garam masala (page 10) .... *4 gms / ²/₃ tsp*
Water .... *800 ml / 4 cups*

Method:

1. Clean and wash the lamb.
2. Heat oil in a *kadhai* (wok), add the whole spices and sauté till they crackle. Add ginger-garlic paste and sauté for a few minutes.
3. Add lamb and chopped onions. Cook on a medium heat till the liquid dries.
4. Add salt, red chilli powder, coriander powder, turmeric powder and carrots.
5. Stir in tomato purée and cook till oil separates.
6. Mix in khoya, brown onion paste, green peas, mushrooms and cashewnuts. Add water to it. Reduce heat, cook on a slow fire till the meat is tender and the curry has thickened.
7. Serve hot, accompanied by steamed rice.

Lamb Dumplings

Serves: 4-5   Preparation time: 30 minutes   Cooking time: 45 minutes

Ingredients:
For the dumplings:
Lamb, minced..*1 kg*
Butter.....................................*50 gms / 3¹/₃ tbs*
Coriander powder ....*4 gms / ³/₄ tsp*
Dried apricots, diced ....*150 gms / ³/₄ cup*
Fennel (*saunf*) powder ....*4 gms / ³/₄ tsp*
Garlic paste (page 10)...............*25 gms / 5 tsp*
Ginger paste (page 10) ....*25 gms / 5 tsp*
Green chillies, finely chopped *2*
Green coriander, finely chopped
.... *10 gms / 2 tsp*
Onions, grated.......................*120 gms /²/₃ cup*
Salt for seasoning
White pepper powder ....*4 gms / ³/₄ tsp*
For the curry:
Oil ....*80 ml /¹/₃ cup*
Bay leaves (*tej patta*) *2*

Cloves (*laung*) *10*
Green cardamoms (*choti elaichi*) *10*
Cinnamon (*daalchini*) sticks..........................*3*
Onion paste (page 10) ....*160 gms / ³/₄ cup*
Ginger paste (page 10) ....*50 gms / 3¹/₃ tbs*
Garlic paste (page 10)............*50 gms / 3¹/₃ tbs*
Red chilli powder ....*10 gms / 2 tsp*
Tomatoes, blanched, deseeded
and chopped ....*350 gms / 1 ³/₄ cups*
Salt for seasoning
Green coriander, chopped .... *15 gms / 1 tbs*
Garam masala (page 10) ....*10 gms / 2 tsp*
Cream ....*10 ml / 2 tsp*
Saffron (*kesar*) strands, dissolved in
15 ml of milk..*a pinch*
Mace (*javitri*) powder ....*4 gms / ³/₄ tsp*
Vetivier (*kewda*) essence ....*3 drops*

Method:
1. Mix all the ingredients for the dumplings (except apricots) until the mixture sticks to the spoon. Season to taste with salt. Divide this mixture into 25 balls.
2. Stuff each meat ball with a diced apricot.
3. Heat oil in a pan, add bay leaves, cloves, cardamoms and cinnamon sticks, sauté over medium heat for 30 seconds.
4. Stir in onion paste, ginger-garlic pastes, sauté for 30 seconds. Add red chilli powder, stir and cook for 3-4 minutes. Mix in tomatoes, stir and cook.
5. Add salt and chopped coriander and simmer over medium heat until the oil separates from the tomato curry.
6. Slip the dumplings into the curry alongwith hot water (1½ cups). Sprinkle garam masala, cover the pan and simmer for 10 minutes.
7. Add cream, the saffron mixture, mace powder and vetivier and remove from heat.
8. Serve hot, accompanied by Naan (page 77).

◄ *Lamb Dumplings*

Lamb with Onions

Serves: 4   Preparation time: 15 minutes   Cooking time: 45 minutes

Ingredients:

Lamb, cut into pieces .... *1 kg*
Butter .... *20 gms / 1¹/₃ tbs*
Button onions .... *300 gms / 1½ cups*
Oil .... *100 ml / 1 ½ cup*
Turmeric (*haldi*) powder .... *6 gms / 1¹/₃ tsp*
Bay leaves (*tej patta*) *3*
Cloves (*laung*) *10*
Cinnamon (*daalchini*) sticks *5*
Red chillies, whole *8*
Green cardamom (*choti elaichi*) *10*
Onions, chopped /sliced .... *200 gms / 1 cup*
Ginger paste (page 10) .... *60 gms / 4 tbs*

Garlic paste (page 10) .... *60 gms / 4 tbs*
Tomatoes, blanched, deseeded, chopped .....
.... *300 gms / 1½ cups*
Garam masala (page 10) .... *12 gms / 2½ tsp*
Coriander powder .... *10 gms / 2 tsp*
Cumin (*jeera*) powder .... *6 gms / 1¹/₃ tsp*
Mace (*javitri*) powder .... *3 gms /²/₃ tsp*
Nutmeg (*jaiphal*) powder .... *a pinch*
Black pepper, crushed .... *10 gms / 2 tsp*
Salt to taste
Green coriander, chopped .... *5 gms / 1 tsp*
Ginger, julienned .... *6 gms / 1¹/₃ tsp*

Method:

1. Blanch the button onions and fry in hot butter for a few minutes.

2. Heat oil in a pan, add turmeric alongwith bay leaves, cloves, cinnamon, whole red chillies, and cardamoms, sauté over medium heat for few seconds until they begin to crackle.

3. Add the onions and sauté until soft and golden in colour. Stir in the ginger and garlic pastes and chopped tomatoes, cook for 5 minutes.

4. Add the lamb pieces, cook for 10-15 minutes over medium heat until a pleasant aroma comes from the lamb. Reduce heat, simmer on low flame and cook until the lamb is tender.

5. Sprinkle with garam masala, coriander powder, cumin powder, mace powder, nutmeg powder and black pepper powder. Season to taste. Add the button onions, stir, cover and cook for 2-3 minutes.

6. Serve hot, garnished with green coriander and julienned ginger, accompanied by Naan (page 77).

Marinated Lamb, Slow Oven Style

Serves: 4   Preparation time: 1½ hours   Cooking time: 1½ hours

Ingredients:

Lamb pieces .... *1 kg*
Yoghurt .... *160 gms / ²/₃ cup*
Salt to taste
Oil .... *160 gms / ²/₃ cup*
Bay leaves (*tej patta*) *2*
Black cardamoms (*bari elaichi*) *3*
Green cardamoms (*choti elaichi*) *8*
Onions, chopped .... *240 gms / 1 cup*
Ginger paste (page 10) .... *45 gms / 3 tbs*

Garlic paste (page 10) .... *45 gms / 3 tbs*
Coriander powder .... *25 gms / 5 tsp*
Turmeric (*haldi*) powder ....*2.5 gms / ½ tsp*
Red chilli powder .... *5 gms / 1 tsp*
Tomatoes, chopped .... *160 gms / ²/₃ cup*
Garlic, chopped .... *20 gms / 4 tsp*
Ginger, shredded .... *20 gms / 4 tsp*
Cumin (*jeera*) powder .... *10 gms / 2 tsp*
Red chillies, whole *4*

Method:

1. Whisk together the yoghurt and salt, marinate the lamb in it for an hour.

2. Heat oil in a *handi* (pot), add bay leaves, both the cardamoms and sauté till they crackle.

3. Add the onions and sauté till light brown. Add ginger and garlic pastes and stir for 4-5 minutes. Stir in coriander, turmeric and red chilli powder.

4. Add the lamb alongwith the excess marinade, bring to a boil, reduce flame and simmer, adding water (3 tsp) at regular intervals. Cook until the lamb becomes tender.

5. Add the tomatoes, chopped garlic, ginger and stir. Then add the cumin and whole red chillies. Cook on low flame till the lamb pieces are tender and evenly coated with the marinade.

6. Remove from heat and serve hot, accompanied by any Indian bread and Boondi Raita (page 81).

Lamb Shanks in Curry

Serves: 4   Preparation time: 30 minutes   Cooking time: 2 hours

Ingredients:

Lamb shanks .... *800 gms / 8*
Oil .... *20 gms / 4 tsp*
Cloves (*laung*) *3*
Green cardamom (*choti elaichi*) *5*
Ginger paste (page 10) .... *30 gms / 2 tbs*
Garlic paste (page 10) .... *30 gms / 2 tbs*
Salt to taste
Yoghurt .... *45 gms / 3 tbs*
Brown onion paste (page 10) .. *30 gms / 2 tbs*
Red chilli powder .... *5 gms / 1 tsp*

Stock .... *750 ml / 3 cups*
Tomato purée .... *120 gms / ½ cup*
Almond paste .... *15 gms / 1 tbs*
Garam masala (page 10) .... *2.5 gms / ½ tsp*
Ginger, julienned .... *5 gm / 1 tsp*
Green coriander, chopped .... *10 gms / 1 tbs*
Saffron (*kesar*) .... *a pinch*
Sweet ittar .... *a few drops*
Dough to seal dish

Method:

1. Heat oil in a *kadhai* (wok) and sauté cloves and cardamoms till they crackle, add the ginger and garlic pastes and sauté till almost dry.

2. Add lamb shanks, salt, yoghurt, brown onion paste and red chilli powder. Stir for 3-5 minutes. Add stock and simmer till meat is tender.

3. Remove shanks into an ovenproof casserole and strain the curry into another pan.

4. Add the tomato purée to the strained curry and cook till the quantity reduces to two-thirds.

5. Stir in the almond paste and the garam masala. Cook for 2-3 minutes. Pour over the shanks.

6. Sprinkle julienned ginger, chopped coriander, saffron (crushed in a few drops of water) and sweet ittar. Seal the casserole with dough and let it simmer for 5 minutes in a preheated (175 °C/350 °F) oven.

7. Open the seal and wipe edges of dish. Transfer to a serving dish (can be served in the same dish).

8. Garnish with chopped coriander and serve hot, accompanied by any Indian bread.

Spicy Lamb Chops

Serves: 4   Preparation time: 15 minutes   Cooking time: 3 hours

Ingredients:

Lamb chops, ... *10 pieces*
Clarified butter (*ghee*) ....*60 ml / 1/3 cup*
Green cardamoms (*choti elaichi*) *8*
Cloves (*laung*) *8*
Cinnamon (*daalchini*) sticks........................*2*
Bay leaves (*tej patta*) *2*
Ginger paste (page 10) ....*40 gms / 2 2/3 tbs*
Garlic paste (page 10) ....*40 gms / 2 2/3 tbs*
Salt to taste
Yoghurt .... *400 gms / 2 cups*
Red chilli powder .... *5 gms / 1 tsp*
Brown onion paste (page 10) ....
....*175 gms / 3/4 cup*

Black pepper powder .... *5 gms / 1 tsp*
Cumin (*jeera*) powder .... *1 gm / 1/5 tsp*
Mace (*javitri*) powder .... *5 gms / 1 tsp*
Green cardamom (*choti elaichi*) powder
.... *1 gm / 1/5 tsp*
Saffron (*kesar*) .... *5 gms / 1 tsp*
Vetivier (*kewda*) essence .... *2 drops*
Milk .... *15 ml / 1 tbs*
Green coriander, chopped .... *5 gms / 1 tsp*
Ginger, julienned .... *10 gms / 2 tsp*

Method:

1. In a pan, heat clarified butter, add the lamb, green cardamoms, cloves, cinnamon, bay leaves, ginger and garlic pastes and salt. Cover and cook on low heat for 30 minutes, stirring occasionally. Uncover and stir-fry for a few minutes.

2. Add yoghurt and continue to stir-fry till the liquid evaporates.

3. Add the red chilli powder, dissolved in water (2 tbs) and stir for a minute. Add brown onion paste dissolved in water (3 tbs) and continue to fry. Add a tablespoon of water when the liquid evaporates, to ensure that the sauce and lamb do not burn.

4. Add half the pepper, cumin and water (6 cups), bring to a boil and cover. Lower the heat, seal the lid with dough and simmer on slow fire for at least 1 hour.

5. Unseal and remove the lamb from the curry. Strain the curry, return to the stove and reduce the curry to pouring consistency.

6. Add the mace, cardamom powder and saffron with vetivier mixed in milk. Cook for about 5 minutes.

7. Pour the sauce over the lamb shanks, garnish with julienned ginger and green coriander and serve hot, accompanied by Lachha Parantha (page 76) or Naan (page 77).

Slow Oven Raan

Serves: 4   Preparation time: 5 hours   Cooking time: 2 hours

Ingredients:

Lamb (leg pieces) .... *1 kg*
Red chilli powder .... *5 gms / 1 tsp*
Salt to taste
Ginger paste (page 10) .... *10 gms / 2 tsp*
Garlic paste (page 10) .... *10 gms / 2 tsp*
Malt vinegar .... *75 ml / 5 tbs*
Spring onions, chopped .... *20 gms / 4-5*
Ginger, chopped .... *160 gms / ²/₃ cup*
Green coriander, chopped .... *10 gms / 2 tsp*
Mint, chopped .... *10 gms / 2 tsp*

Garlic, chopped .... *30 gms / 2 tbs*
Cheese, grated .... *60 gms / ¼ cup*
Black cumin (*shah jeera*) seeds *5 gms / 1 tsp*
Garam masala (page 10) .... *2.5 gms / ½ tsp*
White butter .... *75 gms / 5 tbs*
Onion rings .... *120 gms / ½ cup*
Pineapple, chopped .... *240 gms / 1 cup*
Chaat masala .... *5 gms / 1 tsp*
Green chillies, chopped .... *10 gms / 2 tsp*
Lemon juice .... *15 ml / 1 tbs*

Method:

1. Remove the thigh bone from the leg of lamb. Marinate the lamb in a mixture of red chilli powder, salt, ginger and garlic pastes and half the malt vinegar. Keep aside for 4 hours.

2. Mix onions, ginger, green chillies, coriander, mint and garlic. Add the grated cheese and black cumin. Stuff the leg of lamb with this mixture.

3. Sew the open end of the leg with a needle and thread. Prick the leg with a fork.

4. Arrange the leg in a big baking tray. Pour the remaining malt vinegar and sprinkle garam masala over it.

5. Cover with aluminium foil. Roast in a preheated (175 °C/350 °F) oven for 1½ hours .

6. Heat butter in a pan. Sauté onion rings. Add chopped pineapple and chaat masala and green chillies. Mix well and remove from heat.

7. Slice the leg open and pour the pineapple and onion mixture. Squeeze lemon juice on top and garnish with cucumber slices. Serve hot.

Raan in a Spicy Marinade

Serves: 4-5   Preparation time: 4 ½ hours   Cooking time: 2 hours

Ingredients:

Leg of lamb .... *1 kg*

For the marinade:

Ginger paste (page 10) .... *15 gms / 1 tbs*
Garlic paste (page 10) .... *20 gms / 1¹/₃ tbs*
Malt vinegar .... *100 ml / ½ cup*
Rum (optional) .... *60 ml / ¹/₃ cup*
Salt
Red chilli powder .... *15 gms / 1 tbs*
Yellow chilli powder .... *15 gms / 1 tbs*
Raw papaya paste .... *25 gms /1½ tbs*
Cloves (*laung*), powdered .... *5 gms / 1 tsp*

Cinnamon (*daalchini*), powdered ....
.... *10 gms / 2 tsp*
Yoghurt, hung .... *150 gms / 1 ³/₄ cup*
Butter for basting .... *100 gms / ½ cup*
Chironji paste .... *60 gms / 4 tbs*
Brown onion paste (page 10)   *30 gms / 2 tbs*
Yoghurt .... *100 gms / ½ cup*
Red chilli paste .... *20 gms / 4 tsp*
Garam masala (page 10) .... *15 gms / 1 tbs*
Oil .... *125 ml / ³/₄ cup*

Method:

1. Prick the lamb leg all over with a fork.

2. **For the marinade**, whisk together ginger-garlic pastes, vinegar, rum, salt, red and yellow chilli powder, raw papaya paste, clove powder and cinnamon powder, rub over the leg piece and keep aside for 4 hours.

3. Skewer lamb leg and cook in a tandoor for 15-20 minutes, basting with butter occasionally. Alternatively, bake in a very hot oven till the juices are sealed and meat is lightly coloured.

4. Take lamb leg off the skewer and place on a roasting tray.

5. Blend together, chironji paste, onion paste, yoghurt, red chilli paste and garam masala into fine paste.

6. Cover and seal the tray with an aluminium foil, cook in an oven or on a hot plate for 35-40 minutes.

7. Remove from oven and serve hot, accompanied by Naan (page 77).

SEAFOOD

Coriander flavoured Pomfret (recipe on following page) ▶

Coriander flavoured Pomfret

Serves: 4   Preparation time: 20 minutes   Cooking time: 25 minutes

Ingredients:

Pomfret (300-350 gms each) 4
For the filling:
Green coriander, chopped .... *1 cup*
Green chillies, deseeded and chopped *4*
Ginger, julienned .... *10 gms / 2 tsp*
Garlic cloves, crushed.................................. *10*
Salt to taste
Lemon juice .... *30 ml / 2 tbs*
Oil for frying
For the curry:
Yoghurt .... *500 ml / 2 ½ cups*

Coriander seeds, broiled, pounded
.... *60 gms / 4 tbs*
Salt to taste
Ginger, chopped .... *20 gms /4 tsp*
Coconut cream .... *225 gms*
Onion paste (page 10) .... *20 gms / 4 tsp*
Green cardamom (*choti elaichi*), crushed ... *5*
Bay leaves (*tej patta*) *2*
Peppercorn, freshly crushed .... *15 gms / 1 tbs*
Green chillies, slit *4*
Lemon... *1*

Method:

1. Clean pomfret and debone it keeping it whole. Give slight incisions on the outside.
2. **For the filling**, Mix coriander, green chillies, ginger, garlic, salt and lemon juice together and smear inside and outside of the pomfrets.
3. Heat oil in a pan, lightly fry the pomfrets on both sides and place in shallow oven-proof dish.
4. **For the curry**, whisk together, the yoghurt, coriander seeds, salt, ginger, coconut cream, onion paste, green cardamom, bay leaf, peppercorns, green chillies and juice of the lemon.
5. Pour this mixture over the fish. Cover and bake for 15 minutes.
6. Serve hot, accompanied by steamed rice.

◀ *Picture on preceding page*

Spicy Red Snapper

Serves: 4   Preparation time: 1½ hour   Cooking time: 1½ hour

Ingredients:

Red snapper, (700 gms each) 2

For the marinade:
Ginger paste (page 10) .... *5 gms / 1 tsp*
Garlic paste (page 10) .... *10 gms / 2 tsp*
Salt to taste
Turmeric (*haldi*) powder .... *3 gms / ½ tsp*
Yoghurt, whisked .... *250 gms / 1 ¼ cup*
Lemon juice .... *30 ml / 2 tbs*
Coriander seeds roasted, crushed
.... *10 gms / 2 tsp*

Oil .... *150 ml / ¾ cup*

For the curry:
Onions, chopped .... *150 gms / ¾ cup*
Tomato, chopped.................... *200 gms / 1 cup*
Coriander powder .... *15 gms / 1 tbs*
Red chilli powder .... *10 gms / 2 tsp*
Cashewnut paste .... *15 gms / 1 tbs*
Garam masala (page 10) .... *5 gms / 1 tsp*
Salt to taste
Green coriander, chopped .... *20 gms / 4 tsp*

Method:

1. Clean the fish and make incisions on the flesh.

2. Mix together the ingredients for the marinade. Evenly coat the fish and keep aside for 1 hour.

3. Heat oil in a *kadhai* (wok) and fry the fish evenly till golden brown on both sides. Remove and keep aside.

4. In the same oil, sauté the onions till transparent. Add remaining ingredients (except green coriander) for the curry. Stir-fry for a few minutes, sprinkling water occassionally.

5. In a separate pan, place the fried fish and pour the curry on top. Cover and cook for 10 minutes.

6. Stir in the excess marinade and cook for 5 minutes.

7. Remove to an oven-proof dish, cover and cook for 40 minutes in a moderately hot oven.

8. Serve immediately, accompanied by Naan (page 77).

Fish, Slow Oven Style

Serves: 4   Preparation time: 15 minutes   Cooking time: 30 minutes

Ingredients:

Fish, cut into boneless cubes .... *500 gms*
Oil .... *50 ml / 3 ²/₃ tbs*
Green cardamoms (*choti elaichi*) *4*
Bay leaf (*tej patta*) *1*
Ginger paste (page 10) .... *8 gms / 1 ½ tsp*
Garlic paste (page 10) .... *8 gms / 1 ½ tsp*
Red chilli paste .... *15 gms / 1 tbs*
Coriander powder .... *15 gms / 1 tbs*

Salt to taste
Yellow chilli powder .... *10 gms / 2 tsp*
Poppy seed (*khus khus*) paste . *10 gms / 2 tsp*
Cashewnut paste .... *20 gms / 4 tsp*
Brown onion paste (page 10)   *20 gms / 4 tsp*
Yoghurt ....*250 ml / 1 ¼ cup*
Juice of Lemons *2*

Method:

1. Heat oil in a heavy bottomed pan. Sauté cardamon and bayleaf for a few minutes.

2. Add ginger and garlic pastes and sauté for 1 minute.

3. Add red chilli paste, coriander powder. Stir-fry for another minute and remove from heat.

4. Add all the other ingredients together with the fish except for lemon juice.

5. Transfer this mixture to an oven-proof dish. Cover the dish and seal with dough.

6. Place the dish in an oven at low temperature and allow to cook for 20 minutes. Remove from the oven and sprinkle lemon juice over the fish.

7. Serve hot, accompanied by any Indian bread.

Fish Rolls

Serves: 4   Preparation time: ½ hour   Cooking time: 45 minutes

Ingredients:

Fish (2" × 4" strips). *12*
Butter .... *60 ml / 4 tbs*
Onions, chopped *4*
Green chilli, slit *3*
Turmeric (*haldi*) powder .... *2 gms / ½ tsp*
Ginger, chopped .... *10 gms*

Cream ....*100 ml / ½ cup*
Yoghurt, whisked ....*200 ml / 1 cup*
Fenugreek (*methidana*) seeds
broiled, powdered .... *2 gms / ½ tsp*
Green cardamom (*choti elaichi*) powder
....*2 gms / ½ tsp*

Method:

1. Roll each fish strip and secure with a toothpick.

2. Heat oil in a heavy bottomed pan and sauté onions untill soft.

3. Add green chillies and ginger to the onions and stir-fry for a few minutes.

4. Add turmeric powder, yoghurt, cream, fenugreek and cardamom powder, sauté for 10-15 minutes.

5. Place the fish rolls in the sauce and cook on slow fire/*dum* for 10-15 minutes or until fish is cooked. Remove from heat.

6. Transfer the fish onto a serving dish, remove the toothpicks.

7. Strain the gravy and pour on top of the fish. Serve hot, garnished with green coriander and accompanied by steamed rice.

Fennel flavoured Prawns

Serves: 4   Preparation time: 25 minutes   Cooking time: 35-40 minutes

Ingredients:

Prawns, deveined and shelled *12*
Fennel (*saunf*) seeds
broiled and pounded .... *10 gms / 2 tsp*
Garlic, chopped .... *10 gms / 2 tsp*
Green chillies, deseeded, chopped *5*
Onion paste (page 10) .... *30 gms / 2 tbs*
Lemon juice .... *30 ml / 2 tbs*

Salt to taste
Fennel (*saunf*), chopped .... *25 gms / 5 tsp*
Cream .... *100 ml / ½ cup*
Yoghurt .... *100 ml / ½ cup*
Ginger, chopped .... *5 gms / 1 tsp*
Butter .... *20 gms / 4 tsp*

Method:

1. Heat butter in a pan and sauté the chopped fennel for a few seconds.

2. Add garlic, green chillies and onion paste. Stir-fry for a few minutes.

3. Mix in all the other ingredients and cook for 5-10 minutes. Remove from heat.

4. Place prawns in an oven proof dish, pour the prepared mixture on top. Cover the dish tightly and cook in a preheated (175 °C/350 °F) oven for 15-20 minutes.

5. Remove from the oven. Transfer into a serving platter and serve immediately accompanied by steamed rice and Boondi Raita (page 81).

Prawns Exotica

Serves: 4   Preparation time: 2½ hours   Cooking time: 30 minutes

Ingredients:

Prawns, shelled and deveined.......... *800 gms*
Oil .... *60 ml / ¹/₃ cup*
Mustard (*raee*) seeds .... *3 gms / ½ tsp*
Green cardamoms (*choti elaichi*) *4*
Mace (*javitri*) *4*
Onions, chopped *3*

Garlic, flakes .... *10 gms / 2 tsp*
Ginger, julienned .... *10 gms / 2 tsp*
Green chillies, slit *2*
Salt to taste
Curry leaves *2*
Cream .... *300 ml / 1 ½ cups*

Method:

1. Heat oil in a non-stick pan. Add mustard seeds, cardamom and mace, sauté till they crackle.
2. Add chopped onions, garlic, ginger and slit green chillies. Cook till onions are soft. Add salt.
3. Place the prawns in an oven proof dish and pour the prepared mixture on top of the prawns.
4. Add curry leaves and cream to the mixture.
5. Seal the dish with aluminium foil and cook in a preheated (175 °C/350 °F) oven for 25 minutes.
6. Remove from oven, garnish with chopped coriander and serve hot, accompanied by any Indian bread.

Fish Fillets flavoured with Mustard

Serves: 4   Preparation time: 2½ hours   Cooking time: 20 minutes

Ingredients:

Fish fillets .... *600 gms*

Mustard paste .... *15 gms / 1 tbs*

Red chillies, crushed .... *10 gms / 2 tsp*

Salt to taste

Tomato paste .... *25 gms / 5 tsp*

Lemon juice .... *30 ml /2 tbs*

Onions, chopped *2*

Garlic cloves, chopped *6*

Oil .... *60 ml / 4 tbs*

Method:

1. Mix together the mustard paste, chillies, salt, tomato paste and lemon juice. Marinate the fish fillets in this mixture for 2 hours.

2. Heat oil in a heavy bottomed pan, sauté onion and garlic until transparent.

3. Gently place the fillets in the pan and cook, turning frequently, so that both sides are evenly browned. Pour the remaining marinade alongwith water (½ cup) over the fillets.

4. Cover the pan and leave to simmer for 10 minutes

5. Remove and serve hot, garnished with chopped coriander and accompanied by Lachha Parantha (page 76).

Pomegranate Prawns

Serves: 4   Preparation time: 45 minutes   Cooking time: 15 minutes

Ingredients:

Prawns, (jumbo) 8
Malt vinegar .... *30 ml / 2 tbs*
Salt to taste
Yellow chilli powder .... *2.5 gms / ½ tsp*
Ginger paste (page 10) .... *10 gms / 2 tsp*
Garlic paste (page 10) .... *10 gms / 2 tsp*
Cheddar cheese, grated .... *30 gms / 2 tbs*
Pickled onions, chopped .... *60 gms / ¼ cup*
Green coriander, chopped .... *10 gms / 2 tsp*

Ginger, chopped fine .... *5 gms / 1 tsp*
Cumin (*jeera*) seeds .... *2.5 gms / ½ tsp*
Lemon juice .... *30 ml / 2 tbs*
Peas, fresh .... *120 gms / ½ cup*
White pepper powder .... *2.5 gms / ½ tsp*
Tomato ketchup .... *45 ml / 3 tbs*
Pomegranate (*anaar dana*) seeds,
fresh ....*240 gms / 1 ¼ cup*

Method:

1. Remove the heads from the prawns, slit, devein and pat dry.
2. Mix malt vinegar, salt, yellow chilli powder, ginger and garlic pastes, marinate prawns in it for half an hour.
3. Place each marinated prawn on a separate 10 inch square piece of greased aluminium foil.
4. Boil, drain and crush peas with a rolling pin.
5. Mix together cheese, onion, coriander, ginger, cumin, lemon juice, peas, white pepper powder, tomato ketchup and pomegranate seeds.
6. Top each prawn with this mixture.
7. Grate some more cheese on each and wrap up the foil.
8. Place the wrapped parcels in a baking tray and bake in a preheated oven at (175 °C / 350 °F) for 10-12 minutes.
9. Serve hot, as a snack, accompanied by Mint Chutney (page 10) or as part of the main meal.

VEGETABLES

Slow Oven Cottage Cheese *(recipe on following page)* ▶

Slow Oven Cottage Cheese

Serves: 4   Preparation time: 50 minutes   Cooking time: 25 minutes

Ingredients:

Cottage cheese (*paneer*), cubed .... *500 gms*
Oil .... *50 ml*
Garlic cloves, fried .... *2.5 gms / ½ tsp*
Onions, fried .... *20 gms / 4 tbs*
Chironji paste .... *15 gms / 1 tbs*
Cashewnut paste .... *15 gms / 1 tbs*
Yoghurt .... *250 ml / 1 ¼ cups*

Saffron (*kesar*) .... *a pinch*
Vetivier (*kewda*) essence .... *5 drops*
Yellow chilli powder .... *15 gms / 1 tbs*
Coriander powder .... *20 gms / 4 tsp*
Salt to taste
Green chilli, slit *5*

Method:

* For recipe of *paneer*, turn to page 10.

1. Mix together oil, garlic cloves, onions, chironji paste, cashewnut paste, yoghurt, saffron, vetivier, yellow chilli powder, coriander powder and salt.
2. Marinate the cottage cheese in this mixture for ½ hour.
3. Transfer the cottage cheese alongwith excess marinade in an oven proof dish. Seal with dough or aluminium foil and cook in a preheated (175 °C / 350 °F) for 20 minutes.
4. Remove from oven, garnish with slit green chillies and serve hot, accompanied by steamed rice or Naan (page 77).

◀ *Picture on preceding page*

Curried Green Chillies

Serves: 4   Preparation time: 45 minutes   Cooking time: 30 minutes

Ingredients:

Green chilli, fresh .... *400 gms / 2 cups*
Tamarind (*imli*) .... *100 gms / ½ cup*
Sesame (*til*) seeds .... *5 gms / 1 tsp*
Peanuts .... *15 gms / 1 tbs*
Mustard oil .... *60 ml / 4 tbs*
Mustard (*raee*) seeds .... *2 gms / ½ tsp*
Onion (*kalonji*) seeds .... *2 gms / ½ tsp*

Curry leaves *2*
Ginger-Garlic paste (page 10) *10 gms / 2 tsp*
Cumin (*jeera*) powder .... *5 gms / 1 tsp*
Coriander powder .... *8 gms / 1 ½ tsp*
Red chilli powder .... *5 gms / 1 tsp*
Brown onion paste (page 10)   *20 gms / 4 tsp*
Salt to taste

Method:

1. Soak tamarind in water (½ cup) for ½ hour.

2. Squeeze out, discard pulp and retain extract.

3. Blend sesame seeds and peanuts together to make a fine paste.

4. Heat oil in a *kadhai* (wok), sauté mustard seeds and onion seeds till they crackle.

5. Add curry leaves, stir and add ginger and garlic pastes, sauté for one minute.

6. Stir in the cumin powder, coriander powder, red chilli powder, brown onion paste, salt and the sesame seed-peanut paste.

7. Add the tamarind extract and bring to a boil.

8. Add the green chillies, cover and cook on slow fire for 10-15 minutes or on a hot plate. Remove from heat.

9. Serve hot, accompanied by steamed rice and Boondi Raita (page 81).

Dum Aloo Kashmiri

Serves: 4   Preparation time: 2½ hours   Cooking time: 25 minutes

Ingredients:

Potatoes (medium) 8	Ginger paste (page 10) .... *10 gms / 2 tsp*
Oil .... *100 ml / ½ cup*	Garlic paste (page 10) .... *10 gms / 2 tsp*
Black cumin (*shah jeera*) .... *5 gms / 1 tsp*	Almond paste .... *40 gms / 2 ¾ tbs*
Aniseed .... *5 gms / 1 tsp*	Aniseed .... *5 gms / 1 tsp*
Onions, chopped *2*	Mace (*javitri*) powder .... *3 gms / ½ tsp*
Black cardamom (*bari elaichi*) seeds	Black cumin (*shah jeera*) .... *2 gms / ½ tsp*
pounded .... *5 gms / 1 tsp*	Green cardamom (*choti elaichi*) *4*
Raisins .... *75 gms / 5 tbs*	Cloves (*laung*) *6*
Cashewnuts .... *75 gms / 5 tbs*	Red chilli paste .... *20 gms / 4 tsp*

For the curry:

	Cumin (*jeera*) powder .... *10 gms / 2 tsp*
Onions .... *60 gms / 4 tbs*	Coriander powder .... *15 gms / 1 tbs*
Yoghurt, whisked .... *225 gms / 1 ¼ cups*	Salt to taste
Tomato purée .... *200 gms / 1 cup*	Oil for frying

Method:

1. Peel potatoes, slice off the top. Scoop out the centre. Fry the shell and centres to golden brown. Allow the centres to cool and mash.

2. Heat oil in a *kadhai* (wok). Sauté black cumin and aniseed. Add onions, sauté till transparent. Add the fried potato centres, cardamom powder, raisins and cashewnuts. Stir-fry for few minutes. Season with salt. Keep aside.

3. Stuff the fried shells with the prepared mixture. Keep aside.

4. Heat oil in a thick bottom pan. sauté onions till transparent, add yoghurt, tomato purée, ginger-garlic pastes, almond paste, aniseed, mace, black cumin, cardamoms, cloves, red chilli paste, cumin powder, coriander powder and salt. Stir-fry for 8-10 minutes.

5. Place the stuffed potatoes in the curry, cover the lid and seal with dough. Cook in slow fire for 10 minutes. Remove from heat. Place potatoes in a serving dish, strain the curry and pour on top of the potatoes.

6. Serve immediately, accompanied by Lachha Parantha (page 76).

Tangy Potatoes

Serves: 4   Preparation time: 15 minutes   Cooking time: 40 minutes

Ingredients:

Potatoes (small) .... *600 gms*	Cumin (*jeera*) powder .... *10 gms / 2 tsp*
Oil .... *100 ml / ½ cup*	Cashewnut paste (optional) .... *30 gms / 2 tbs*
Onions, chopped .... *20 gms / 4 tsp*	Cloves (*laung*) powder .... *3 gms / ½ tsp*
Cumin (*jeera*) seeds .... *10 gms / 2 tsp*	Cinnamon (*daalchini*) powder .... *a pinch*
Turmeric (*haldi*) powder .... *3 gms / ½ tsp*	Salt to taste
Red chilli powder .... *5 gms / 1 tsp*	Yoghurt .... *400 gms / 2 cups*

Method:

1. Peel the potatoes and soak in water.
2. Heat oil (1 tbs) in a pan and sauté onions till brown.
3. Heat oil in a *kadhai* (wok), sauté cumin seeds till they crackle, add turmeric powder, red chilli powder and cumin powder alongwith water (½ cup).
4. Mix in all the remaining ingredients and cook for 5 minutes.
5. Add the peeled potatoes to the curry, seal the lid with dough. Cook on low flame for 30-35 minutes.
6. Remove from heat, transfer to a serving dish and serve hot, accompanied by Naan (page 77) and Boondi Raita (page 81).

Stuffed Bottle Gourd

Serves: 4 Preparation time: 1½ hour Cooking time: 25-30 minutes

Ingredients:

Bottle Gourd (450 gms each) 2
Ginger-Garlic paste (page 10) *15 gms / 1 tbs*
Lemon juice .... *30 ml / 2 tbs*
Red chilli powder .... *5 gms / 1 tsp*
Turmeric (*haldi*) powder ....*2 gms / ½ tsp*
Salt to taste
Clarified butter (*ghee*)........... *100 gms / ½ cup*

Green coriander, chopped .... *10 gms / 2 tsp*
Green chillies, chopped 4
Garam masala (page 10) .... *5 gms / 1 tsp*
Almond, chopped 10
Raisins, chopped .... *10 gms / 2 tsp*
Salt to taste
Lemon..*1*

For the filling:

Clarified butter (*ghee*)............... *60 gms / 4 tbs*
Onion, finely chopped............ *50 gms / ¹/₃ cup*
Cottage cheese (**paneer*) .... *150 gms / ¾ cup*
Potatoes, boiled, peeled, grated ....
.... *300 gms /1 ½ cup*
Ginger, finely chopped .... *10 gms / 2 tsp*

For the curry:

Clarified butter (*ghee*) .... *30 gms / 2 tbs*
Tomatoes, blanched, puréed, strained ....
.... *400 gms / 2 cups*
Brown onion paste (page 10) *25 gms / 5 tsp*
Red chilli powder .... *5 gms / 1 tsp*
Garam masala (page 10) .... *5 gms / 1 tsp*

Method:

   * For recipe of *paneer*, turn to page 10.
1. Wash, peel and cut the ends of the bottle gourd. Core the length of each and keep aside.
2. Mix all ingredients for the marinade and rub into the bottle gourd inside and out, keep aside for 1 hour.
3. Heat clarified butter in a pan. Fry marinated bottle gourd evenly and keep aside to cool.
4. **For the filling**, heat clarified butter in a *kadhai* (wok) and sauté onions, add cottage cheese. Stir-fry for few minutes, add grated potatoes alongwith the remaining ingredients, sauté for another 10 minutes and remove from heat. Allow the mixture to cool.
5. Stuff each bottle gourd with the prepared mixture.
6. **For the curry**, heat clarified butter in a pan, mix all ingredients and bring to a boil.
7. Place the stuffed bottle gourd in the curry, cover the pan and seal edges with dough. Cook on slow fire for 6-7 minutes.
8. Remove from heat, slice the bottle gourd into 1½ inch thick rounds, arrange on a serving platter and pour the curry on top.
9. Serve hot, accompanied by Khasta Roti (page76).

◀ *Stuffed Bottle Gourd*

Baked Aubergines

Serves: 4-5   Preparation time: 10 minutes   Cooking time: 45 minutes

Ingredients:

Aubergines (*baigan*), small, oval 20
Oil .... *120 ml /²/₃ cup*
Red chillies, whole *12*
Cumin (*jeera*)seeds .... *10 gms / 2 tsp*
Black peppercorn .... *6 gms / 1¹/₃ tsp*
Green cardamoms (*choti elaichi*) *10*
Cinnamon (*daalchini*) sticks.......................... *5*
Bay leaf (*tej patta*) *1*

Cloves (*laung*) *10*
Malt vinegar .... *60 ml / 4 tbs*
Onion paste (page 10) .... *150 gms / ³/₄ cup*
Ginger paste (page 10) .... *40 gms / 2²/₃ tbs*
Garlic paste (page 10) .... *40 gms / 2²/₃ tbs*
Turmeric (*haldi*) powder .... *5 gms / 1 tsp*
Salt to taste

Method:

1. Trim the stems of the aubergines. Slit open each aubergine lengthwise, without disjoining it from the stem.

2. In a pan, heat oil (1 tbs). Add the red chillies, cumin seeds, black peppercorn, green cardamoms, cinnamon sticks, bay leaf, cloves and sauté over medium heat for 5-6 minutes. Cool and grind finely.

3. Mix in vinegar to make a fine paste.

4. Heat a little oil in a pan. Fry the aubergines, a few at a time, for 5-6 minutes or until they are half cooked. Remove from heat and keep aside.

5. In the same pan, heat remaining oil, add the onion paste and sauté over medium heat for 10-12 minutes, until the paste is lightly coloured.

6. Add the ginger and garlic pastes, turmeric powder and the ground spice paste. Stir and cook over medium heat for 4-5 minutes.

7. Add the salt and hot water (²/₃ cup), cook until the water evaporates and the oil separates from the sauce.

8. Arrange the fried aubergines in the sauce, stir very carefully, cover and cook over a low flame or in a slow oven for 3-4 minutes.

9. Serve hot, accompanied by any Indian bread.

Spiced Cauliflower

Serves: 4-5   Preparation time: 10 minutes   Cooking time: 45 minutes

Ingredients:

Cauliflower, small, whole 5	Garlic paste (page 10) .... *25 gms / 5 tsp*
Oil for frying	Garam masala (page 10) .... *10 gms / 2 tsp*
Onions, chopped .... *200 gms / 1 cup*	Yoghurt, whisked .... *200 gms / 1 cup*
Cashewnuts .... *100 gms / ½ cup*	Salt to taste
Green cardamoms (*choti elaichi*) 6	Butter .... *30 gms / 2 tbs*
Turmeric (*haldi*) powder .... *5 gms / 1 tsp*	Lemon juice .... *15 ml / 1 tbs*
Red chilli powder .... *10 gms / 2 tsp*	Mace (*javitri*) powder .... *3 gms / ²/₃ tsp*
Ginger paste (page 10) .... *25 gms / 5 tsp*	

Method:

1. Wash, clean and remove the stems of the cauliflower.
2. Heat oil in a *kadhai* (wok), deep fry each cauliflower over medium heat until almost cooked.
3. In the same oil, fry onions and cashewnuts (saving a few for garnishing), grind to a fine paste.
4. Heat oil (5 tbs) in a pan, add cardamoms, sauté for a few seconds. Add turmeric powder, red chilli powder, ginger-garlic pastes and garam masala, cook for 30 seconds.
5. Add onions-cashewnut paste and whisked yoghurt, cook for 10 minutes on low heat and season to taste with salt.
6. Arrange the fried cauliflower in a baking dish and pour the curry over each cauliflower. Bake in a moderate oven of 175 °C (350 °F) for 10 minutes.
7. Garnish with fried cashewnuts, dot with melted butter and sprinkle lemon juice and mace powder. Serve hot, accompanied by Khasta Roti (page 76).

Spicy Lentils

Serves:4   Preparation time: 15 minutes   Cooking time : 30 minutes

Ingredients:

Lentils *(arhar daal)* .... *240 gms / 1¼ cup*
Salt to taste
Yellow chilli powder .... *5 gms / 1 tsp*
Garlic paste (page 10) .... *15 gms / 1 tbs*
Cream .... *120 gms / ½ cup*
Yoghurt .... *240 gms / 1¼ cup*

Clarified butter *(ghee)* .... *120 gms / ½ cup*
Garlic, chopped .... *15 gms / 1 tbs*
Cumin *(jeera)* seeds .... *2.5 gms / ½ tsp*
Onions, chopped .... *120 gms / ½ cup*
Red chillies, whole *4*
Pepper to taste

Method:

1. Pick, clean and wash lentils.
2. Boil with water (1 lt), salt and yellow chilli powder till they become tender.
3. Add garlic paste and cook further for 10 minutes.
4. Add cream, yoghurt and clarified butter (¼ cup). Cook again for 10 minutes, stirring frequently so that the clarified butter is incorporated into the lentils.
5. Heat the remaining clarified butter in a pan. Sauté the chopped garlic, cumin and onions for 2 minutes.
6. Add whole red chillies and sauté till brown. Add this mixture to the cooked lentils and stir for 5-10 minutes.
7. Sprinkle pepper, top with a knob of butter and serve hot, accompanied by any Indian bread.

Pumpkin and Peas

Serves: 4   Preparation time: 45 minutes   Cooking time: 40 minutes

Ingredients:

Red pumpkin (cut into 1" square) .... *800 gms*
Peas .... *150 gms / ¾ cup*
Oil .... *60 ml / 4 tbs*
Fenugreek (*methi dana*) seeds *10 gms / 2 tsp*
Garlic, chopped .... *10 gms / 2 tsp*
Onion paste (page 10) .... *60 gms / 4 tbs*

Cumin (*jeera*) powder .... *6 gms / 1 tsp*
Coriander powder .... *5 gms / 1 tsp*
Red chilli powder .... *7 gms / 1 ½ tsp*
Garam masala (page 10) .... *5 gms / 1 tsp*
Salt to taste
Yoghurt .... *250 gms / 1¼ cup*

Method:

1. Heat oil in a *kadhai* (wok), sauté fenugreek seeds till they begin to crackle.
2. Add garlic and onion paste and sauté till golden brown.
3. Mix in the cumin powder, coriander powder, red chilli powder, garam masala, salt, and yoghurt. Stir well and sauté for 10-15 minutes.
4. Add the pumpkin and peas, mix well.
5. Cover and cook in a preheated (175 ºC / 350 ºF) oven or cook on slow fire for 25-30 minutes.
6. Remove from heat and serve hot, accompanied by Lachha Parantha (page 76) and Boondi Raita (page 81).

ACCOMPANIMENTS & DESSERTS

Assorted Indian Breads (*recipes on following pages*) ▶

Lachha Parantha

Serves: 4   Preparation time: 1½ hours   Cooking time: 30 minutes

Ingredients:

Flour .... *480 gms / 2 ²/₃ cups*
Fennel (*saunf*) .... *10 gms / 2 tsp*
Salt to taste
Milk ....*240 ml / 1¼ cup*

Water .... *120 ml / ²/₃ cup*
Clarified butter (*ghee*) ....*180 ml / ¾ cup*
Clarified butter to shallow fry

Method:
1. Pound fennel with a pestle.
2. Sieve flour and salt together. Make a well in the flour and pour in milk and water. Mix gradually and knead into a dough. Cover with moist cloth and keep aside for 10 min.
3. Melt ¹/₃ of the clarified butter, add to the dough, kneading constantly to make it soft and smooth.
4. Add pounded fennel and knead again for 5 minutes.
5. Divide into 12 equal balls, dust lightly, roll into 6" discs. Apply (1 tsp) clarified butter evenly over one side.
6. Make a radial cut and fold disc into a narrow conical shape. Place flat side of the cone on palm and twist palms together in a round movement to compress dough into a thick flat round (*pedha*). Dust with flour, roll it out into an 8 inch disc. Refrigerate for an hour on butter paper.
7. Heat griddle and shallow fry both sides over low heat till golden. Serve hot, as an accompaniment to any dish.

Khasta Roti

Serves: 4-5   Preparation time: 25 minutes   Cooking time: 10-15 minutes

Ingredients:
Whole wheat flour............. *500 gms / 2½ cups*
Salt to taste
Carom (*ajwain*) seeds .... *15 gms / 1 tbs*

Sugar .... *12 gms / 2½ tsp*
Water ....*300 ml / 1½ cups*

◀ *Laccha Parantha (picture on preceding page)*

Method:
1. To the sieved flour, add salt, sugar and carom seeds. Knead into a hard dough with water. Cover with a moist cloth and keep aside for 15 minutes.
2. Divide the dough into 10 equal portions and roll into balls. Dust and roll into 10 cm discs. Prick with a fork evenly.
3. Bake the rotis for 8-10 minutes in an preheated (175 °C / 350 °F) oven or till light brown in colour.
4. Serve hot, as an accompaniment to any curry dish or with any yoghurt preparation.

Naan

Serves: 4-5   Preparation time: 3 hours   Cooking time: 20 minutes

Ingredients:

Flour .... *500 gms / 2½ cups*
Salt to taste
Baking soda.................................. *1 gm / ¼ tsp*
Baking powder............................ *5 gms / 1 tsp*
Egg *1*

Sugar .... *10 gms / 2 tsp*
Milk .... *50 ml / 3⅓ tbs*
Clarified butter (*ghee*)/Oil.......... *25 ml / 5 tsp*
Onion (*kalonji*) seeds .... *3 gms / ⅓ tsp*
Melon (*magaz*) seeds .... *5 gms / 1 tsp*

Method:
1. Sieve the flour, salt, baking soda and baking powder into a bowl. Add enough water to make a hard dough.
2. Whisk egg, sugar and milk in a bowl and knead into the dough to make it soft and smooth. Cover with moist cloth, keep aside for 10 minutes.
3. Add oil, knead and punch the dough, cover again with moist cloth, keep aside for 2 hours to allow the dough to rise.
4. Heat the oven to 175 °C (350 °F).
5. Divide the dough into 6 balls and place on a lightly floured surface. Sprinkle onion and melon seeds, flatten the balls slightly, cover and keep aside for 5 minutes.
6. Flatten each ball between the palms to make a round disc, then stretch on one side to form an elongated oval.
7. Place on a greased baking tray and bake for 2-3 min.
8. Serve hot, as an accompaniment to any curry dish.

◀ *Naan (picture on page 75)*

Exotic Chicken Biryani

Serves: 4-5 Preparation time: 50 minutes Cooking time: 1 hour

Ingredients:

Chicken, cleaned, cut into 8 pieces .... *1 kg*
Rice, basmati or any long grain variety
.... *500 gms / 2½ cups*
Yoghurt, whisked .... *600 gms / 3 cups*
Saffron (*kesar*), dissolved in milk ...... *0.5 gms*
Milk .... *100 ml / ½ cup*
Cream .... *50 ml / ¼ cup*
Mint leaves, chopped .... *10 gms / 2 tsp*
Green coriander, chopped .... *10 gms / 2 tsp*
Water .... *4 litres*
Bay leaves (*tej patta*) *2*
Green cardamoms (*choti elaichi*) *10*
Cloves (*laung*) *10*

Salt to taste
Black cardamoms (*bari elaichi*) *2*
Cinnamon (*daalchini*) sticks *4*
Black cumin (*shah jeera*) seeds
.... *6 gms / 1⅓ tsp*
Onions, sliced .... *100 gms / ½ cup*
Ginger paste (page 10) .... *40 gms /2 ⅔ tbs*
Garlic paste (page 10) .... *40 gms / 2⅔ tbs*
Lemon juice .... *10 ml / 2 tsp*
Butter, unsalted .... *150 gms / ¾ cup*
Mace (*javitri*) powder .... *5 gms / 1 tsp*
Red chilli powder .... *10 gms / 2 tsp*

Method:

1. Wash the rice and soak it for at least half an hour.
2. Divide yoghurt in 2 equal portions. Add saffron milk and cream to 1 portion alongwith mint and coriander. Keep aside.
3. Preheat the oven to 150 °C (300 °F).
4. Boil water (4 lts) in a large pan and add one bay leaf, 2 green cardamoms and 2 cloves. Add the rice and salt to taste, boil for a few minutes until the rice is half cooked. Drain the rice with the whole spices and keep aside.
5. Heat butter in a pan, add the remaining whole spices and black cumin, sauté over medium heat until the cumin begins to crackle. Add onions and sauté until golden brown. Add ginger-garlic pastes and red chillies, stir for 15 seconds. Add the chicken and salt to taste, cook further for 3-4 minutes.
6. Add the second portion of plain yoghurt alongwith water (200 ml), bring to a boil, lower heat and simmer until the chicken is almost done. Stir in lemon juice.
7. Grease a large baking dish, spread half the chicken, sprinkle half of the saffron-yoghurt mixture on top, cover with half of the rice. Repeat the layering process and place a moist cloth over the final layer. Cover the dish and seal with dough.
8. Bake in slow oven for 20-25 minutes. Remove and serve hot, garnished with fried almonds and accompanied by Boondi Raita (page 81).

◀ *Exotic Chicken Biryani*

Boondi Raita

Serves: 4-6   Preparation time: 10-15 minutes   Cooking time: 20 minutes

Ingredients:

Gramflour (*besan*), sifted ..... *100 gms / ½ cup*
Salt to taste
Baking powder .... *⅓ tsp*
Water ....*60-75 ml / 4-5 tbs*
Oil/Clarified butter (*ghee*) for frying
Yoghurt .... *400 ml / 2 cups*

Cumin (*jeera*) seeds, roasted, crushed ....
.... *7 gms / 1 ½ tbs*
Pistachio. raw, blanched, chopped
.... *30 gms / 2 tbs*
Green coriander, chopped .... *30 gms / 2 tbs*

Method:

1. For the *Boondi*, mix together the gramflour, salt (¼ tsp) and baking powder in a bowl, gradually add water and whisk to a smooth batter, having consistency of heavy cream.

2. Heat oil / clarified butter in a deep-frying pan. Pour about 2 tbs of batter at a time into a frying spoon with several holes, hold the spoon above the pan and press the batter through the holes with your fingers. They will froth in the hot oil, then rise to the surface. Fry until crisp and golden in colour. Remove on paper towels to drain. Repeat the process for all the batter.

3. In a bowl of warm water, put 2-3 tbs of *boondi*, leave to soften, then gently squeeze between palms to remove excess water, set aside.

4. Whisk together in a bowl, yoghurt, salt to taste, cumin seeds, nuts and coriander until smooth and creamy.

5. Stir in the soaked *boondi*. Garnish with the reserved crispy *boondi* and sprinkle cayenne pepper, serve at room temperature'or chilled.

◀ *Boondi Raita*

Rasgoola

Serves: 8   Preparation time: 2 hours   Cooking time: 50 minutes

Ingredients:

Whole milk ....*2 lts / 8 cups*
Lemon juice .... *60 ml / 4 tbs*
Water ....*2 lts / 8 cups*
Sugar ....*1.5 kg*

Cornstarch (dissolved in 2 tbs water)
.... *15 gms / 1 tbs*
Vetivier (*kewda*) essence .... *2.5 gms / ½ tsp*

Method:

1. Take milk in a heavy bottomed pan, bring to a frothing boil, reduce heat. Add lemon juice and stir. This will make the milk curdle and the cheese to separate from the whey. If the cheese does not separate add another tablespoon of lemon juice. Remove from heat and set aside for 10 minutes.

2. Pour the cheese-whey mixture into a moist cheese cloth, gather the four corners of the cloth and rinse it under tap water for about 10 minutes. Gently twist the cloth to squeeze out excess water. Tie up the corners and hang for 20 minutes to allow all excess water to drain.

3. Meanwhile, mix the water and sugar in a pan, bring to a boil, stirring continuously until the sugar dissolves completely. Cook on high heat for 3-4 minutes, remove from heat and set aside.

4. Unwrap the cheese on a clear work surface and crumble it repeatedly till it becomes fluffy and smooth.

5. Collect all the cheese into one big portion and coat with a thin layer of oil from all sides. Divide into 16 portions and shape each into a smooth ball.

6. Reheat the sugar syrup, bring to a boil and slide in the prepared balls. Increase heat and boil continuously for about 20 minutes adding cornstarch with ¼ cup water after 4 minutes of boiling. Thereafter ¼ cup of water to maintain the consistency of syrup. Take care to add the water directly into the syrup and not on the balls. Remove from heat.

7. Allow to cool for 10 minutes, sprinkle the vetivier essence. Leave to soak the rasgoolas at room temperature for atleast 4 hours before consumption. Serve chilled or at room temperature, 2 rasgoolas per person with a few tablespoons of syrup.

◀ *Rasgoola*

INDEX

Accompaniments

Boondi Raita 81
Exotic Chicken Biryani 79
Khasta Roti 76
Lachha Parantha 76
Naan 77

Chicken

Chicken Drumsticks 27
Chicken Drumsticks in a unique marinade 15
Chicken Handi 19
Chicken in Spinach Purée 25
Chicken Mince Rolls 12
Saffron Chicken 27
Slow Oven Chicken with a hint of Mint 17
Slow Oven Tandoori Chicken 12
Spicy Chicken Curry 28
Tamarind flavoured Chicken Curry 21
Tangy Chicken 23

Desserts

Rasgoola 83

Lamb

Boneless Lamb in Tomato purée 33
Lamb Curry 31
Lamb Dumplings 35

Lamb Shanks in curry 41
Lamb with Onions 37
Marinated Lamb, Slow Oven Style 39
Raan in a Spicy Marinade 46
Slow Oven Lamb Steaks 30
Slow Oven Raan 45
Spicy Lamb Chops 43

Seafood

Coriander flavoured Pomfret 48
Fennel flavoured Prawns 55
Fish Fillets flavoured with Mustard 57
Fish Rolls 53
Fish, Slow Oven Style 51
Pomegranate Prawns 58
Prawns Exotica 56
Spicy Red Snapper 49

Vegetarian

Baked Aubergines 69
Curried Green Chillies 61
Dum Aloo Kashmiri 63
Pumpkin and Peas 74
Slow Oven Cottage Cheese 60
Spiced Cauliflower 71
Spicy Lentils 73
Stuffed Bottle Gourd 67
Tangy Potatoes 65